MW00593756

THE MINI BOOK OF

SAINTS

by Diana von Glahn

RUNNING PRESS

Philadelphia • London

Library of Congress Control Number: 2008928491

ISBN 978-0-7624-3433-6

Running Press Book Publishers
2300 Chestnut Street
Philadelphia, PA 19103–4371

Visit us on the web!
www.runningpress.com

Contents

What Is A Saint?

What is a saint? A very simple, dictionary-type definition would be someone who has lived such a holy and virtuous life, we can be sure they are in Heaven. While those who are named as saints don't necessarily include everyone in Heaven, they have undergone some sort of test that proves to those of us on Earth that they are, in fact, among the lucky souls in Heaven.

On a basic level, saints are our brothers and sisters in faith who lived the same difficult life that we lead—some even more difficult—and were still able to follow in Christ's example. They are, for us, proof that striving to live a life following Christ's example is not impossible. These men and women show us that you don't need to be perfect to be holy. You just need to love.

That's why we pray to saints, and why saints are made patrons.

Think about it this way: say you have a friend who works at a place where you really want to work. It would be smart to ask him or her to put in a good word for you so you can get a job there, too. That's like praying to saints for those of us who want to get to Heaven. They're already there, you see, and they know the struggles we're enduring here on Earth. So, if we find a saint whose life or struggles were similar to ours, or who inspires us, we pray to them, asking them to put in a good word for us with our Heavenly boss.

In a similar vein, if you struggle with something difficult here on Earth, you can pray to a saint who struggled with the same thing, and ask him or her to ask God to send a little strength your way. Like praying to St. Augustine for an increase of chastity, or St. Rita, to help bring about peace in a very difficult situation. They can be our spiritual mentors, offering us their examples as someone who got through similar challenges. They can also be our advocates in prayer, as we ask God for the virtues we need to endure trials on Earth.

On these pages, we've presented to you more than 90 of some of the most popular saints in the canon. There are many, many more, and there are hundreds of books about and by saints to help inspire you and move you as you make your way to Heaven.

St. Agnes

Patron saint of betrothed couples,
chastity, and rape victims

DIED: c.304 in Rome, Italy

FEAST DAY: January 21

St. Agnes was thirteen when she was killed for refusing to betray her promise to remain a virgin for Christ. She is often seen holding a lamb, as a symbol of her virginal innocence. On her feast day, two lambs are blessed and from their wool are made the *palliums* (stoles) that the Pope gives to newly appointed archbishops.

St. Alphonsus Liguori

Patron saint of confessors and theologians

BORN: **September 27, 1696 in Marianelli, Italy**

DIED: **August 1, 1787 in Nocera**

FEAST DAY: **August 1**

A child prodigy, St. Alphonsus received his legal degree at age 16! He left the law for the Church at age 29.

A prodigious writer, St. Alphonsus wrote 111 works on spirituality and theology. His best known works include *The Glories of Mary*, *The Practice of the Love of Jesus Christ*, and *The Way of the Cross*.

St. Aloysius Gonzaga

Patron saint of teens and students

BORN: March 9, 1568 in
Lombardy, Italy

DIED: June 20, 1591 in Rome, Italy

FEAST DAY: June 21

St. Aloysius received his first Communion from St. Charles Borromeo (page 44). He decided he wanted to be a priest after reading a book about Jesuit missionaries in India.

Visit the Church of St. Ignatius of Loyola in Rome, where St. Aloysius is buried.

St. Ambrose

Patron saint of beekeepers
and candlemakers

BORN: c.340 in Trier, Germany

DIED: April 4, 397 in Milan, Italy

FEAST DAY: December 7

When the bishop of Milan died, Ambrose replaced him—even though he wasn't baptized! His gentle and influential speech led him to be called the "Honey-Tongued Doctor."

Visit the Basilica Sant'Ambrogio in Milan, Italy.

St. Andrew the Apostle

Patron saint of fishermen and Scotland

DIED: Greece

FEAST DAY: November 30

This first apostle and brother of St. Peter, St. Andrew was martyred on a saltire—an x-shaped cross. Some say he preached for two days, from the cross, before he died.

This saint's relics are kept at the church of St. Andres at Patras, Greece.

St. Andrew Kim Taegon & Companions

Patron saint of Korean clergy

BORN: August 22, 1822 in Korea

DIED: September 16, 1846

FEAST DAY: September 21

FIRST NATIVE KOREAN CATHOLIC PRIEST

During the Joseon Dynasty, Christianity was suppressed in Korea, and many Christians were executed. St. Andrew was tortured and beheaded, one of thousands who were martyred for their faith during this time.

St. Anselm

Patron saint of scholastics

BORN: Aosta, Italy

DIED: 1109 in Canterbury, England

FEAST DAY: April 21

A famous philosopher and theologian, St. Anselm originated the ontological argument. He is most often remembered for his attempts to prove the existence of God.

St. Anthony of Padua

Patron saint of various Italian cities

BORN: 1195 in Lisbon, Portugal

DIED: June 13, 1231

FEAST DAY: June 13

This saint, popular among Italians and those who seek things they've lost, was canonized (made a saint) less than one year after his death. Also known as the "Hammer of Heretics," St. Anthony was so eloquent in his defense of the faith. After his death, when his body was exhumed, his tongue was found to be completely incorrupt!

Visit St. Anthony's Basilica—La Basilica di sant'Antonio di Padova—in Padua, Italy, or check out the St. Anthony Shrine in Cincinnati, Ohio. For a beautifully produced film about this saint, watch *Saint Anthony, The Miracle Worker of Padua*.

St. Augustine

Patron saint of theologians,
printers, and brewers

BORN: November 13, 354 in Tagaste,
Algeria

DIED: August 28, 430 in Hippo

FEAST DAY: August 28

The wild child of saints, St. Augustine
is the ultimate prodigal son. After
years of struggling against his mother's
constant prayers for him, and often
praying, "God, give me chastity and
continence . . . but not just now," he

eventually learned enough to convince himself that, as he said in his famous *Confessions*, "Our hearts were made for You, O Lord, and they are restless until they rest in You."

St. Augustine's *Confessions*, often called the first Western autobiography, has inspired many to take a good look at their lives and strive for holiness. Visit the church of San Pietro in Ciel d'Oro, in Pavia, Italy, to see this saint's final resting place.

St. Bartholomew

Patron saint against nervous disorders
and of tanners

DIED: **Albanopolis, Armenia**

FEAST DAY: **August 24**

St. Bartholomew, one of the Twelve
Apostles of Christ, was flayed alive and
beheaded, so he is often portrayed as
holding human skin or a tanner's knife!

St. Bartholomew's relics are kept in a
few places: at the Church of St. Bartholomew
(San Bartolomeo all'Isola), on Tiber Island in

Rome; in Canterbury Cathedral in England; and at the Cathedral of Bartholomew in Frankfurt. In the Sistine Chapel, an image of St. Bartholomew, holding his skin, can be found in Michelangelo's painting, *The Last Judgment*. The face on the skin is said to be that of Michelangelo, himself!

St. Bede the Venerable

Patron saint of lectors

BORN: 672 in Wearmouth, England

DIED: May 25, 735

FEAST DAY: May 25

Although the road to sainthood includes three steps—Venerable, Blessed, and Saint—Bede's title comes from a mistranslation of the inscription on his tomb, which read "Here lie the venerable bones of Bede," but was mistranslated as "Here lie the bones of Venerable Bede."

St. Bede's work, *The Ecclesiastical History of the English People,* earned him the title of the Father of English History. Bede the Venerable is buried in Durham Cathedral in northeast England.

St. Benedict

BORN: c.480 in Narsia, Italy

DIED: March 21, 547 in Monte
Cassino, Italy

FEAST DAY: July 11

St. Benedict's *Rule* was written for lay-men, to help them live as fully as the life presented in the Gospels.

St. Benedict founded the monastery at Monte Cassino, in Italy—the roots of the Church's monastic system. It was bombed in 1944, during World War II, but rebuilt and consecrated in 1964.

St. Bernadette Soubirous

BORN: January 7, 1844 in Lourdes, France

DIED: April 16, 1879 in Nevers, France

FEAST DAY: April 16

St. Bernadette's incorrupt body can still be seen at the St. Gildard Convent in Nevers, where she died.

Visit the shrine at Lourdes, France, and be sure to watch the Oscar-winning movie, *The Song of Bernadette*.

St. Bernardine
of Siena

Patron saint of advertisers and those
with lung problems

BORN: 1380 in Massa di Carrara,
Italy

DIED: 1444 in Aquila, Italy

FEAST DAY: May 20

St. Bernardine was so eloquent when
he preached that he became patron
saint of advertisers.

St. Blaise

Patron saint of those with throat illnesses

DIED: c.316

FEAST DAY: February 3

On the feast of St. Blaise, Catholic priests around the world bless the throats of their parishioners. This tradition comes from the fact that St. Blaise saved a child who was choking on a fish bone.

St. Brigid of Ireland

Patron saint of Ireland

BORN: 453 in County Louth, Ireland

DIED: 523 in Kildare, Ireland

FEAST DAY: February 1

St. Brigid founded the first convent in Ireland, the Convent of Cill-Dara (now Kildare)—which means "church of the oak" in Gaelic.

To visit the traditional burial place of Ireland's patron saints, Patrick, Columba, and Brigid, you'll have to go to Down Cathedral in Down-patrick, Ireland.

St. Bridget of Sweden

Patron saint of Europe and Sweden

BORN: c.1302 in Uppsala, Sweden

DIED: July 23, 1373 in Rome, Italy

FEAST DAY: July 23

St. Bridget was a pious young girl, born of a wealthy family. She married at age 13, and gave birth to eight children, including St. Catherine of Sweden. After her husband's death, she renounced her title and founded her order at Vadstena.

Visit the Abbey of Vadstena, where St. Bridget is buried, in Sweden.

St. Casimir

BORN: 1458 in Cracow, Poland

DIED: 1484 in Lithuania

FEAST DAY: March 4

St. Casimir was Prince of Poland, the second son of King Casimir IV, yet he rejected the extravagant lifestyle of royalty, often choosing to sleep on the floor rather than on his royal bed.

St. Catherine Labouré

Patron saint of those who wear the
Miraculous Medal

BORN: May 2, 1806 in Fain-les-
Moûtiers, France

DIED: December 31, 1876 in
Enghien-Reuilly

FEAST DAY: November 28

As a novice, Catherine Labouré
received numerous visions of the
Blessed Virgin, culminating in the Virgin's request that Catherine have a
medal made based on the apparitions,
now known as the Miraculous Medal.

St. Catherine's incorrupt body can still be seen, just below the altar where she first met Mary, at the Chapel of Our Lady of the Miraculous Medal on the Rue de Bac, in Paris. In the U.S., you can visit the Miraculous Medal Shrine in Philadelphia, PA or in Perryville, Missouri.

St. Catherine of Siena

Patron saint of firefighters

BORN: March 25, 1346 in Siena, Italy

DIED: April 29, 1380

FEAST DAY: April 29

St. Catherine was a mystic who was in constant conversation with God. She persuaded the Pope to return to Rome after a prolonged stay at Avignon, France, and she received invisible stigmata that were only visible after her death.

St. Catherine's book, *The Dialogue*, is a series of questions posed to God. For a wonderful fictionalized account of her life, see Louis De Wohl's *Lay Siege to Heaven*. Visit Siena, Italy, to see where the saint lived, or to see the Basilica of San Domenico, where the saint's head is kept.

St. Cecilia

Patron saint of musicians

DIED: c.117

FEAST DAY: November 22

St. Cecilia was martyred during the early centuries of the Church. After surviving an overheated bathhouse, she was sentenced to be beheaded.

St. Cecilia's body was buried just as it was found, and statues were made of her in her death pose. You can still find these statues throughout Rome. Visit her in the Roman catacombs. You can also visit the church of Santa Cecilia in Trastevere in Rome.

St. Charles Borromeo

Patron saint of seminarians, catechists, and catechumens

BORN: October 2, 1538 in Novara, Italy

DIED: November 2, 1584 in Milan

FEAST DAY: November 4

St. Charles was the son of Margaret Medici—sister of Pope Pius IV and a member of one of the most notorious families in Italian history! Unlike most well-known members of this family, St. Charles was humble, holy, and unselfish. He made great reforms in his diocese, established seminaries, founded the Confraternity of Christian Doctrine (CCD), and was active in bringing lapsed Catholics back to the church.

Visit Milan Cathedral—the largest Gothic cathedral in Italy—to see the remains of this holy man.

St. Charles Lwanga
& Companions

Patron saint of converts, torture victims,
and African Catholic Youth Action

BORN: 1865 in Bulimu, Uganda

DIED: 1886 in Namugongo, Uganda

FEAST DAY: June 4

The 22 martyrs of Uganda were killed in horrific ways, all because their life conflicted with the lifestyle of the cruel King Mwanga. As they died, many of them smiled and pointed heaven-ward with excitement, saying to the priest who wept for them, "Why are you so sad? This is nothing to the joys you have taught us to look forward to."

In Kampala, Uganda, the Cathedral of St. Mary in Rubaga, or Rubaga Cathedral, is located on the same spot as the murderous King Mwanga. In Namugongo, there is a shrine right on the place where St. Charles Lwanga was martyred.

St. Clare

Patron saint of eye disease and television

BORN: July 16, 1194 in Assisi, Italy

DIED: August 11, 1253

FEAST DAY: August 11

St. Clare, whose name in Italian is Chiara, is patron saint of television because toward the end of her life, when she was too ill to attend Mass, she was miraculously able to see and hear it on the wall of her bedroom. The Eternal Word Television Network

(EWTN), based in Birmingham, Alabama, was founded by Mother Angelica, a Poor Clare.

Assisi is one of the most spiritually rich cities in all of Italy. For St. Clare alone, there are countless sites to visit, including the Basilica of di Santa Chiara, where her remains can be seen; the Church of Our Lady of the Angels, where she took the veil of religious life from St. Francis of Assisi; and the church of San Damiano, where she died.

St. Dominic

BORN: 1170 in Burgos, Spain

DIED: August 4, 1221 in Bologna,
Italy

FEAST DAY: August 8

Founder of the Order of the Friars
Preachers (Dominicans, OFP)

St. Dominic once became discouraged,
because no matter how hard he fought
against heresies, they still remained.
He saw the Blessed Virgin, who

showed him a wreath of roses, representing the rosary. She told him to pray it daily, and to teach all who would listen, and that eventually, the true faith would win out. Today, Dominicans still wear a long—15 decade—rosary as part of their habit.

St. Dominic is buried at the Basilica of San Domenico in Bologna, Italy. For more information about the rosary, read St. Louis de Montfort's *The Secret of the Rosary*, or to learn how to pray it see *The Rosary, Chain of Hope*, by Father Benedict Groeschel.

St. Dymphna

Patron saint of those suffering
from mental illness

FEAST DAY: **May 15**

When Dymphna's father went mad
from the loss of his wife, he tried to
find a new wife who looked just like
his first one. Eventually, he chose his
daughter. When she escaped, he
hunted her down and killed her.

The Church of St. Dymphna, in Geel, Belgium,
houses the relics of this saint, who was killed
there.

St. Elizabeth of Hungary

BORN: July 7, 1207 in Presburg, Hungary

DIED: November 17, 1231 in Marburg

FEAST DAY: November 17

Despite her marriage at age 14 to Louis IV of Thuringia, she spent her life serving the poor and sick.

St. Elizabeth's relics can be visited at Elizabeth Church (Elisabethkirche) in Marburg, Germany.

St. Elizabeth of Portugal

Patron saint of brides and charitable workers

BORN: 1271 in Aragon, Spain

DIED: July 4, 1336 in Estremoz

FEAST DAY: July 4

This Spanish princess eventually became Queen of Portugal as a teenager. As a widow, she gave away her property to the poor and became a Poor Clare at a monastery she founded at Coimbra.

Visit this saint's incorrupt body at the Carmelite Convent where she died in Coimbra, Portugal.

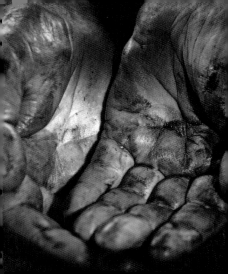

St. Faustina Kowalska

Patron saint of mercy

BORN: August 25, 1905 in
Glogowiec, Poland

DIED: October 5, 1938 in Krakow

FEAST DAY: October 5

St. Faustina obtained numerous visions
of Christ during her life, many of
which she chronicled in her autobiography,
Divine Mercy in my Soul. Archbishop
Karol Wojtyla (the future Pope
John Paul II) was instrumental in pro-

viding a good translation of her book, which led to her eventual canonization during his papacy.

St. Faustina's life is chronicled in a Polish film entitled *Faustina*, which was produced in 2005. Her writings led to the institution of the Chaplet of Divine Mercy and Divine Mercy Sunday, the Sunday after Easter, during which the world celebrates God's Mercy. If you can't visit the shrine to this saint in Krakow, Poland, visit the National Shrine of Divine Mercy in Stockbridge, MA.

St. Francis of Assisi

Patron saint of animals, families,
and San Francisco, CA

BORN: 1181 in Assisi, Italy

DIED: October 4, 1226 in
Portiuncula, Italy

FEAST DAY: October 4

Although St. Francis is often portrayed
as an animal lover, his message and
way of life meant so much more. He
preached absolute poverty, purity, and
peace, all toward the goal of living in
imitation of Christ. In 1224, he
received the stigmata, which remained
for the remaining two years of his life.

There are numerous books and movies about St. Francis. Be sure to check out the classic book, *The Flowers of St. Francis* and the Italian film, *St. Francis*.

St. Francis de Sales

Patron saint of authors, journalists,
and the deaf

BORN: 1567 in France

DIED: 1622

FEAST DAY: January 24

St. Francis' book, *Introduction to the Devout Life*, was written in an attempt to introduce the uneducated to the love of God. In it, he said that the test of one's faith was revealed in his actions.

St. Francis is buried at the Basilica of the Visitation at Annecy, France.

IMMIGRATION

APPROVED

11 MAR 20..

St. Francis Xavier Cabrini

Patron saint of immigrants

BORN: July 15, 1850 in Sant'Angelo Losigiano, Italy

DIED: December 22, 1917 in Chicago, Illinois

FEAST DAY: December 22

FIRST AMERICAN CITIZEN SAINT

Sent to New York City as a missionary, Mother Cabrini founded many homes and orphanages. She became an American citizen in 1909.

St. Gabriel, Archangel

Patron saint of communications workers
and post offices

FEAST DAY: September 29

The Archangel Gabriel is best known as God's messenger. He appeared to Daniel (Daniel 8:16-26), Zachary (Luke 1:11-20), and the Virgin Mary, to announce the conception of her Son (Luke 1:25-38).

St. Genevieve

Patron saint of Paris, France

BORN: c.422 in Nanterre, France

DIED: 512 in Paris, France

FEAST DAY: January 3

St. Genevieve is often represented with a loaf of bread, because of her generosity toward the poor.

Visit the Shrine of St. Genevieve at the Eglise Saint Etienne du Mont in Paris, France, near the Pantheon.

St. George

Patron saint of England

DIED: c.304

FEAST DAY: April 23

St. George, who was a Roman soldier and a Christian killed for his faith, is often shown killing a dragon. His chivalrous behavior made him a favorite in Europe.

Pope St. Gregory the Great

BORN: c.540 in Rome, Italy

DIED: March 12, 604 in Rome

FEAST DAY: September 3

One of the few popes given the title "Great," Pope St. Gregory collected the melodies and chants that are now known as Gregorian Chant.

The Benedictine monastery of Solesmes in France is one of the most amazing places to hear Gregorian chant.

St. Ignatius of Loyola

Patron saint of Spain and soldiers

BORN: 1491 in Loyola, Spain

DIED: July 31, 1556 in Rome, Italy

FEAST DAY: July 31

St. Ignatius was a page in the Spanish court of Ferdinand and Isabella. He longed to be a brave knight, but he was laid out by a battle wound. During his recuperation, the only books available to him were *The Golden Legend* and *The Life of Christ*. After reading these, his whole life, and the lives of billions afterward, changed.

St. Ignatius gave up his dreams of fruitless battle by hanging up his sword before the altar of the Virgin of Montserrat. You can visit Montserrat today, just outside of Barcelona, Spain. In Rome, the Church of the Gesù— Chiesa del Sacro Nome di Gesù—is the mother church of the Jesuits, and the last resting place of St. Ignatius.

Sts. Isaac Jogues & John de Brebeuf

Patron saint of the Americas, Canada

BORN: 1607 in Orleans, France/1593 in Normandy

DIED: 1646 in Ossernenon/1649

FEAST DAY: October 19

St. Isaac and St. John were two North American martyrs who were killed by Iroquois during a peace mission.

The National Shrine of the North American Martyrs, in upstate New York, celebrates the lives of these courageous men.

St. James the Apostle

Patron saint of pharmacists

BORN: Palestine

DIED: c.44

FEAST DAY: May 3

Stabbed to death by King Herod Agrippa, St. James' relics are perhaps some of the most visited relics in the world. The pilgrimage to Santiago de Compostela draws more than 100,000 people from around the world.

St. Jerome

Patron saint of Bible scholars and librarians

BORN: 347 in Strido, Dalmatia

DIED: 419

FEAST DAY: September 30

St. Jerome was secretary to Pope Damasus I, who commissioned him to revise the Latin text of the Bible. The result is the Vulgate translation of the Bible.

Visit St. Jerome's relics at Rome's Basilica di Santa Maria Maggiore.

Sts. Joachim & Anne

Patron saints of grandparents

FEAST DAY: July 26

Saints Joachim and Anne are the parents of the Virgin Mary, Earthly grandparents of Jesus.

St. Joan of Arc

Patron saint of France and soldiers

BORN: January 6, 1412 in
Greux-Domremy, France

DIED: May 30, 1431 in
Rouen, France

FEAST DAY: May 30

The impact this teenage shepherdess
had on France, and the world, is monu-
mental. At 16, she moved a frightened
king of France to reconquer his king-
dom. At 17, she was leading armies of
men. At 19, she was burned at the stake.

Joan's life is as inspirational as it was heroic, and it has been retold in countless films and books. Mark Twain's *Joan of Arc: Personal Recollections* is not only remarkably accurate, but beautifully told. Despite Twain's strong feelings against institutional religion, he spent 12 years researching for this book, which he considered to be his most important and best work. For a gloriously beautiful movie, check out Carl Dreyer's 1928 silent film, *The Passion of Joan of Arc*.

St. John the Apostle

DIED: c.101 in Ephesus
(modern Turkey)

FEAST DAY: December 27

Known as the Beloved Disciple, John
was the only Apostle of Jesus who
stood at the foot of the Cross.

Visit the Basilica of St. John, at Ephesus,
where you can see the saint's tomb.

St. John the Baptist

Patron saint of monastic life

DIED: c.30

FEAST DAY: June 24

St. John the Baptist was Jesus' cousin, born of Mary's cousin Elizabeth. He was beheaded by King Herod.

It is believed that the head of John the Baptist is held at the Basilica of San Silvestro in Capite, in Rome.

St. John Chrysostom

Patron saint of lecturers

BORN: c.347 in Antioch, Asia Minor

DIED: 407

FEAST DAY: September 13

John earned the title *Chrysostom*, which means *golden mouthed*, because he was such a talented orator.

Many of this saint's writings can still be found today in bookstores. Read this saint's writings, such as *On Living Simply* or his many homilies, and see for yourself why he earned the title of "golden tongue."

St. John Nepomucene Neumann

Patron saint of Catholic schools and Philadelphia, PA

BORN: 1811 in Prachititz, Bohemia (Czech Republic)

DIED: 1860 in Philadelphia, PA

FEAST DAY: January 5

SECOND AMERICAN SAINT, ORGANIZED THE FIRST 40 HOURS DEVOTION IN THE U.S.

St. John Neumann spoke at least twelve languages, including his native German and Bohemian and the scholarly lan-

guages of Greek and Latin. In order to better minister to the many American immigrants, he learned Italian, Spanish, English, French, and Gaelic.

Visit the National Shrine of St. John Neumann at 1019 North Fifth Street in Philadelphia, PA.

St. Josemaria Escriva

BORN: January 9, 1902 in Barbastro, Spain

DIED: June 26, 1975

FEAST DAY: June 26

St. Josemaria founded Opus Dei, an organization dedicated to helping people in all walks of life to follow Christ.

St. Josemaria Escriva's many writings include *The Way*, *Christ is Passing By*, *The Furrow*, and *The Forge*.

St. Joseph

Patron saint of workers and fathers

DIED: First century

FEAST DAY: March 19

Some say that the tradition of burying a statue of St. Joseph outside a house you want to sell has been traced to St. Teresa of Avila. She prayed to the saint for assistance in finding land for her convents and buried medals of the saint to consecrate land in his name.

St. Joseph of Cupertino

Patron saint of air travelers

BORN: June 17, 1603 in Cupertino, Italy

DIED: September 18, 1663 in Ossimo, Italy

FEAST DAY: September 18

From a young age, Joseph received ecstatic visions that left him staring into space. Eventually, no punching, pinching, or pricking would revive him of these ecstasies—which could be triggered by church bells or the mere mention of God or the Blessed Virgin. It is even said that he would levitate during his ecstasies, hence his patronage of air travelers.

St. Juan Diego

Patron saint of lay apostles

BORN: 1474 in Tlayacac, Mexico

DIED: May 30, 1548

FEAST DAY: December 9

Juan Diego had only recently converted to Christianity when he met a lovely woman, dressed like an Aztec princess, on Tepeyac Hill. She asked him to tell the city's bishop to build a church on that hill, but he was afraid that he would be ignored. After three attempts, he finally convinced the bishop by bringing him a poncho (or *tilma*) full of beautiful roses in the dead of winter. And on his *tilma*, was imprinted an image of the Virgin Mary that can still be seen today.

Visit the Basilica of Our Lady of Guadalupe in Mexico City to see the miraculous *tilma* of Juan Diego. This garment, featuring one of Mexico's most revered images, is made of cactus fibers, yet has survived six centuries and a bomb! Visit the National Shrine of Juan Diego in Mexico City.

St. Kateri Tekakwitha

Patron saint of the environment

BORN: 1656 in Auriesville, New York

DIED: April 17, 1680 in
Caughnawaga, Canada

FEAST DAY: July 14

FIRST NATIVE AMERICAN SAINT

St. Kateri was the daughter of a Christian Algonquin woman captured by the Iroquois and married to a Mohawk chief. She took her name, the Mohawk pronunciation of Catherine, as her baptismal name, after Catherine of Siena (page 40).

Visit the National Shrine of St. Kateri in Fonda, New York or her birthplace at the Auriesville Martyrs Shrine in New York.

St. Katharine Drexel

Patron saint of racial justice

BORN: 1858 in Philadelphia, PA

DIED: 1955

FEAST DAY: March 3

Katharine Drexel was known as the world's richest nun, and she devoted every penny she had to bettering the lives of African Americans and Native Americans. Today, the Sisters of the Blessed Sacrament continue her legacy of reaching out to the poor.

Visit the National Shrine of St. Katharine Drexel at 1663 Bristol Pike, in Bensalem, PA.

St. Lawrence

Patron saint against fire,
of comedians, and cooks

BORN: Huesca, Spain

DIED: August 10, 258

FEAST DAY: August 10

St. Lawrence was condemned to die a
slow, cruel death because of his faith—
he was tied to the top of an iron grill
over a fire. True to his cheerful nature,
the saint joked, "Turn me over, I'm
done on this side!"

The church of San Lorenzo in Panisperna in Rome was built over the place of St. Lawrence's martyrdom. San Lorenzo Fuori la Mura (St. Lawrence Outside the Walls) houses his remains and a stone on which his body was laid after his death, while the gridiron on which St. Lawrence was martyred is kept beneath the altar at the church of San Lorenzo, in Lucina.

Pope St. Leo the Great

Patron saint for a holy death

BORN: c.400 in Tuscany, Italy

DIED: April 11, 461 in Rome, Italy

FEAST DAY: November 10

Pope St. Leo encountered one of history's greatest villains—Attila the Hun—when the bully marched on Rome. But he didn't turn away from the challenge—he met Attila at the city's gates and told him to leave. As Leo spoke, Attila saw a man in priestly robes standing behind Leo and bearing a sword. The man told Attila if he didn't leave, he'd kill him himself. Many say that was the day Attila the Hun met St. Peter.

"Virtue is nothing without the trial of temptation, for there is no conflict without an enemy, no victory without strife."

St. Louis-Marie Grignion de Montfort

Patron saint of preachers

***

BORN: **January 31, 1673 in Montfort, France**

DIED: **April 28, 1715 in Saint Laurent sur Sevre, France**

FEAST DAY: **April 28**

***

St. Louis wrote some of the most beloved books about devotion to the Virgin Mary, including *The Secret of the Rosary* and *True Devotion to Mary*.

St. Lucy

Patron saint against blindness

BORN: c.283 in Syracuse, Italy

DIED: c.304

FEAST DAY: December 13

St. Lucy is often pictured as holding a cup with . . . her eyes in it! Legend tells us that her eyes were torn out because she refused to marry a pagan or succumb to prostitution. She was eventually stabbed to death.

Visit the church of San Geremia in Venice to view this saint's relics.

St. Luke the Apostle

Patron saint of artists, bookbinders,
and painters

DIED: c.74 in Greece

FEAST DAY: October 18

St. Luke was born to non-Jewish parents, and was one of the earliest converts. His Gospel is the longest of the
four, and has a special emphasis on
prayer and joyfulness.

It is believed that St. Luke's remains are
housed at the Basilica di Santa Giustina in
Padua, Italy.

St. Margaret Mary Alacoque

Patron saint of devotees
of the Sacred heart

BORN: July 22, 1647 in
L'Hautecourt, France

DIED: October 17, 1690

FEAST DAY: October 13

St. Margaret Mary received many
apparitions of Christ and His Blessed
Mother, but one special one resulted in
the devotion to Christ's Sacred Heart.

St. Margaret Mary's incorrupt body can be seen
at the Shrine at Paray-le-Monial in France.

St. Maria Goretti

Patron saint of youth and victims of rape

BORN: October 16, 1890 in
Corinaldo, Italy

DIED: July 6, 1902

FEAST DAY: July 6

One of the youngest saints, St. Maria
died at age 12 after a 19-year-old
farmhand attempted to rape and stab
her. She forgave him as she died, and
he later converted and was present at
her canonization.

St. Mark the Evangelist

Patron saint of lawyers and notaries

DIED: April 25, 68 in Alexandria

FEAST DAY: April 25

St. Mark is often represented by a lion. He is believed to have been the apostle who ran away when Jesus was arrested on the night of His Passion.

It is said that St. Mark's relics are housed at the beautiful Basilica of St. Mark in Venice, Italy.

St. Martha

DIED: c.80

FEAST DAY: July 29

In Luke's Gospel, Martha busies herself in serving Jesus while her sister Mary sits at His feet. When she complains, Jesus tells her that Martha is a little too worried about things that distract her from Him. She's a great example for those of us who are a little too busy for our own good!

The Gospels tell us that Jesus visited Martha, her sister Mary, and their brother Lazarus at least three times—Luke 10:38-42; John 11:1-53; and John 12:1-9.

St. Martin of Tours

Patron saint of beggars and soldiers

BORN: c.316 in Upper Pannonia, Hungary

DIED: November 8, 397 in Tours, France

FEAST DAY: November 11

A soldier of the Roman imperial army, and a Christian, this holy man did his best to live his faith. One day, he saw a beggar sitting on the side of the road. Since he had nothing to give him, he cut his robe in half and gave it to the man. Later, he had a vision of Christ wearing the cloak.

St. Mary Magdalene

Patron saint of penitent sinners
and women

FEAST DAY: July 22

Called the penitent, Mary Magdalene
was a notorious sinner. When she met
Jesus, she felt sorrow for her way of life,
and wept at his feet, bathing them in
her tears and wiping them dry with her
hair. She was present at Christ's crucifixion and was the first of his followers
to see Him after His resurrection.

Mary, Mother of God

Queen of Angels, refuge of sinners

BORN: Jerusalem

FEAST DAY: January 1

Considered the greatest saint of all, Mary is the mother of Jesus Christ. She encouraged Him to perform His first miracle at the marriage at Cana (John 2:3-5), and she witnessed His brutal Passion and crucifixion.

Shrines to the Blessed Virgin Mary can be found all around the world.

St. Matthew the Apostle

Patron saint of bankers, money managers

FEAST DAY: **September 21**

As a tax collector, St. Matthew was hated by most people in his town. But when this man met Jesus, his whole life changed, and Christ reminded everyone that he came, "not for the just, but sinners."

St. Maximilian
Mary Kolbe

Patron saint of drug addiction and prisoners

BORN: January 7, 1894 in Zdunska
Wola, Poland

DIED: August 14, 1941 in Auschwitz

FEAST DAY: August 14

St. Maximilian was sent to Auschwitz
for protecting Jewish refugees during
the Nazi invasion of Poland. There, he
volunteered to die in place of a married man with children who had been

sentenced to die for attempting to escape the prison camp. St. Maximilian died of a lethal injection of carbonic acid. The man he saved survived the camp and spent the next fifty years paying homage to the saint.

Leonardo Defilippis portrays this heroic martyr of charity in the movie *Maximilian: Saint of Auschwitz.*

St. Michael, Archangel

Patron saint of artists, a holy death,
and police officers

FEAST DAY: September 29

Michael's name, which means "Who is like to God," is said to have been the battle cry of the angels as they fought Satan and his followers.

It is said that, after receiving a rather harrowing vision, Pope Leo XIII penned this prayer to St. Michael: St. Michael the Archangel, defend us in battle. Be our safeguard against the wickedness and snares of the devil. May God rebuke him, we humbly pray, and do Thou, oh Prince of the Heavenly Host, cast into Hell Satan and all the evil spirits who prowl about the world seeking the ruin of souls. Amen.

St. Monica

Patron saint of abuse victims, alcoholics, and housewives

BORN: 322 in Tagaste, Algeria

DIED: 387 in Ostia, Italy

FEAST DAY: August 27

St. Monica was the mother of St. Augustine (page 26), who prayed fervently for the conversion of her son and abusive husband. She was once told by a priest, "It is not possible that the son of so many tears should perish." She died the year of her son's baptism.

St. Nicholas of Myra

Patron saint of children

DIED: c.346 in Myra, Turkey

FEAST DAY: December 6

Because of St. Nicholas' generosity to the poor, and special protection of the innocent, his legend became the foundation for today's Santa Claus.

In Bari, Italy, the Basilica di San Nicola (Basilica of St. Nicholas) houses St. Nicholas' tomb.

St. Nicholas of Tolentino

Patron saint of sailors and animals

BORN: 1245 in Sant'Angelo, Italy

DIED: September 10, 1305 in
Tolentino, Italy

FEAST DAY: September 10

St. Nicholas had a great devotion to
the Holy Souls in Purgatory, and often
prayed and fasted for them.

Visit the Basilica di San Nicola a Tolentino in
Tolentino, Italy.

St. Norbert

Patron saint of peace and Bohemia

BORN: c. 1080 in Xanten, Germany

DIED: June 6, 1134 in Magdeburg, Germany

FEAST DAY: June 6

St. Norbert joined the Benedictines as a career move, but a near-death experience made him take his vows so seriously, he founded an order that brought reform to the Church.

Visit the Strahov Monastery in Prague, founded by St. Norbert, which now houses his relics.

St. Padre Pio da Pietrelcina

BORN: May 25, 1887 in Pietrelcina, Italy

DIED: September 23, 1968

FEAST DAY: September 23

St. Pio, or Padre Pio as he is lovingly known, miraculously received the stigmata—the wounds of Christ—on September 20, 1918. After World War II soldiers brought home stories of this saintly man. People from around the world traveled to his monastery to offer their confessions to him. He was miraculously able to read the consciences of those who stood before him. He could bilocate (appear in two places at the same time), levitate, and heal by touch. He had regular bouts with the devil, as well.

Visit Padre Pio's monastery, Santa Maria della Grazie, in Pietrelcina, Italy, or go to New York City, where, right next to Madison Square Garden, lies the Padre Pio Shrine, inside of the gorgeous church of St. John the Baptist.

St. Patrick

Patron saint of Ireland

BORN: c.387 in Scotland

DIED: c.461 in Ireland

FEAST DAY: March 17

St. Patrick used the shamrock to explain the doctrine of the Trinity— that in the unity of God, there are three persons: the Father, the Son, and the Holy Spirit.

Lough Derg, in Ireland, known as St. Patrick's Purgatory, is a popular place of pilgrimage and retreat.

St. Paul

Patron saint of publishers and authors

BORN: c.3 in Tarsus, Turkey

DIED: c.65 in Rome

FEAST DAY: June 29

St. Paul was a Roman soldier who regularly killed Christians, until one day, he was thrown from his horse and told that by persecuting Christians, he was persecuting Christ, Himself.

Visit St. Paul Outside the Walls—San Paolo fuori le Mura—in Rome.

St. Peter

Patron saint of fishermen, First Pope

DIED: c.64 in Rome, Italy

FEAST DAY: June 29

St. Peter was crucified upside-down, because he felt unworthy to die in the same manner as Christ.

Visit St. Peter's Basilica at Vatican City in Rome. You can also visit the Church of St. Peter in Chains—San Pietro in Vincoli—where the chains that held the first Pope captive can still be seen.

St. Peter Claver

*Patron saint of African-Americans
and against slavery*

BORN: 1581 in Verdu, Spain

DIED: September 8, 1654 in
Cartagena, Colombia

FEAST DAY: September 9

St. Peter ministered unceasingly to the
African slaves he met at Cartagena,
Columbia, the principle slave market
of the New World. He loved the slaves
and fought valiantly for the abolition
of the slave trade.

Visit the Cloister, Museum, and Church of St.
Peter Claver in Cartagena, Colombia.

St. Philip Neri

Patron saint of the U.S. Army
Special Forces

BORN: July 22, 1515 in
Florence, Italy

DIED: May 27 1595

FEAST DAY: May 26

"Cheerfulness strengthens
the heart and makes us
persevere in a good life.
Therefore the servant of
God ought always to be in
good spirits."

Although St. Philip Neri is often portrayed in a very somber manner, he was actually quite cheerful and playful.

Look past those somber statues of this fabulous saint, and read more about his cheerful nature in Francis X. Connolly's book, *St. Philip of the Joyful Heart* or Antonio Gallonio's *The Life of St. Philip Neri.*

St. Raphael,
Archangel

FEAST DAY: **September 29**

Raphael's name means "God heals."
He appears in the Book of Tobit in the
Bible.

St. Rita of Cascia

Patron saint of peacemakers
and impossible cases

BORN: 1386 in Roccaparena, Italy

DIED: May 22, 1457 in Cascia

FEAST DAY: May 22

St. Rita received the stigmata—a thorn from Christ's crown of thorns—in the center of her forehead as the result of her prayer that she share in Christ's suffering.

For an updated telling of her life, check out Father Michael Di Gregorio's, *The Precious Pearl: The Story of Saint Rita of Cascia*, or watch the Italian movie *Saint Rita*.

St. Rose of Lima

Patron saint against vanity, of florists, and Latin America

BORN: 1586 in Lima, Peru

DIED: April 15, 1668

FEAST DAY: August 23

FIRST SAINT BORN IN THE AMERICAS

Isabel was such a beautiful baby, her family called her Rose, and the name stuck. But as Rose grew older, she grew more humble, and had no desire to be admired.

The shrine to St. Rose of Lima can be found in the Church of Santo Domingo in Lima, Peru; St. Martin of Porres is also buried there.

St. Scholastica

Patron saint of nuns and storms

BORN: 480

DIED: 543

FEAST DAY: February 10

St. Scholastica's twin brother was St. Benedict, the father of Western Monasticism. Because of their religious vows, they could only see each other about once a year. On one occasion, Scholastica begged him to stay with her to continue their conversation about spiritual matters, but he had to return to the monastery. So after she said a short prayer, a storm raged outside, making it impossible for Benedict to leave. Scholastica died three days later.

St. Sebastian

Patron saint of archers, athletes,
and soldiers

BORN: Narbonne, Gaul (France)

DIED: c.288 in Rome, Italy

FEAST DAY: January 20

St. Sebastian was a Roman soldier,
despite being a Christian. When his
faith was discovered, he was shot with
arrows and left to die. He is often seen
tied to a post, with arrows penetrating
his body.

St. Simon Stock

Patron saint of Bordeaux, France

BORN: c.1165 in Aylesford, England

DIED: May 16, 1265 in Bordeaux, France

FEAST DAY: May 16

St. Simon received an apparition from the Virgin Mary during which she presented him with the brown scapular.

Visit the Carmelites at Aylesford Priory in Kent, England.

St. Stephen

DIED: c.33

FEAST DAY: December 26

St. Stephen was a deacon, and the first martyr, being stoned to death.

Visit the Basilica of St. Lawrence Outside the Walls in Rome, where St. Stephen's remains are said to be kept.

St. Teresa of Avila

Patron saint of Spain and against headaches

BORN: March 28, 1515 in Avila, Spain

DIED: October 4, 1582 in Alba de Tormes

FEAST DAY: October 15

Teresa of Avila was a forceful personality and zealous woman, and she used her gifts to reform her order and found many houses. Both Thérèse of Lisieux and Mother Teresa were named after her. She often said, "Zeal for Your house will consume me."

St. Teresa's *Interior Castle, The Way of Perfection*, and autobiography are must-reads to get to know this amazing firebrand of a woman.

St. Thérèse of Lisieux

Patron saint of florists and missionaries

BORN: January 2, 1873 in Alcon, France

DIED: September 30, 1897 in Lisieux, France

FEAST DAY: October 1

Through her "Little Way," this young French nun helps millions of people grow in holiness through the little challenges we face in our daily lives. Novena—nine-day prayers—to this saint usually ask her to send flowers from heaven as a sign that she has heard the prayers of the faithful. She rarely disappoints.

Thérèse's autobiography, *Story of A Soul*, provides such a wonderful window into this nun's life and "Little Way." The film *Thérèse* presents a lovely vision of the saint's life. Visit the Shrine to St. Thérèse at Lisieux, France. In the U.S., shrines to this popular saint can be found in countless cities, including Pueblo, CO; San Antonio, TX; and Royal Oak, MI.

St. Thomas the Apostle

Patron saint against doubt
and of architects

DIED: c.72 in India

FEAST DAY: July 3

The term "doubting Thomas" comes
from the story of this Apostle who,
when told of Christ's resurrection, said
that he wouldn't believe it until he put
his fingers into the holes in Christ's
hands and the hole in his side. When
Christ met him the following day, he
exclaimed, "My Lord, and My God!"

St. Thomas Aquinas

Patron saint of Catholic universities, book-sellers, and philosophers

BORN: c.1225 in Naples, Italy

DIED: 1274

FEAST DAY: January 28

St. Thomas has been called one of the most influential theologians of all time. His prolific writings, encompassing more than 60 works, include *Summa Theologica* and the songs *Tantum Ergo Sacramentum* and *Adoro te Devote*.

St. Thomas Becket

Patron saint of clergy

BORN: December 21, 1118 in London, England

DIED: December 29, 1170 in Canterbury, England

FEAST DAY: December 29

After challenging King Henry II on the rights of the Church, St. Thomas was murdered in Canterbury Cathedral.

Geoffrey Chaucer's *The Canterbury Tales* tells the story of pilgrims on their way to the shrine of St. Thomas Becket. Visit Canterbury Cathedral in England.

St. Valentine

Patron saint of love

DIED: c.268 in Rome

FEAST DAY: February 14

Visit St. Valentine Basilica in Terni, Italy, to see one of the two saints believed to be behind the popular custom of St. Valentine's Day.

St. Veronica

Patron saint of photographers

FEAST DAY: July 12

During his Way to the Cross, Christ met Veronica, a holy woman who took her veil and wiped Christ's face; an image of Christ remained on the towel. Her name is believed to come from the Latin words *vera* and *icon*, meaning *true image*.

At St. Peter's Basilica, at Vatican City, a statue of St. Veronica sits below a loggia, which houses a scrap of material with the imprint of a bearded man, believed to be Veronica's veil. This and the other relics that surround this part of the Basilica, are shown to the public on the fifth Sunday of Lent.

St. Vincent de Paul

Patron saint of hospital workers, lepers,
and volunteers

BORN: 1581 near Ranquine, France
DIED: 1660 in Paris
FEAST DAY: September 27

St. Vincent's main virtue was charity,
and everything he did was in service
for the poor.

Visit the Eglise Saint Vincent de Paul in Paris,
France, to see the incorrupt body of St. Vin-
cent. His heart is kept in the Miraculous Medal
Shrine on the Rue de Bac, also in Paris.

Guardian Angels

FEAST DAY: October 2

Many believe that each of us has a guardian angel whose mission it is to shepherd us through life and help us achieve holiness. Be sure to talk to yours and ask him for guidance!

Angel of God, my Guardian dear, to whom God's love entrusts me here, ever this day be at my side, to light and guard, to rule and guide. Amen.

PHOTOGRAPHY

This book has been bound using handcraft methods and Smyth-sewn to ensure durability.

The dust jacket and
interior were designed by
JOSH MCDONNELL.

The text was written by
DIANA VON GLAHN.

The text was edited by
T.L. BONADDIO.

The text was set in
BEMBO & HELVETICA.